A Life that Counts

A Life that Counts

10 READY-TO-USE MEETINGS

Editor: Steve Adams

First published in 2004 by Spring Harvest Publishing Division and Authentic Media

10 09 08 07 06 05 04   7 6 5 4 3 2 1

Authentic Media, 9 Holdom Avenue, Bletchley, Milton Keynes, Bucks, MK1 1QR, UK
and PO Box 1047, Waynesboro, GA 30830-2047, USA
www.authenticmedia.co.uk

*The right of Steve Adams to be identified as the Editor of this Work
has been asserted by him in accordance with the
Copyright, Designs and Patents Act 1988.*

British Library Cataloguing in Publication Data

A catalogue record for this book is available from the British Library

ISBN 1-85078-601-1

Cover design by 4-9-0 ltd
Typeset by Temple Design
Print Management by Adare Carwin

Contents

Introduction

This collection of 10 meeting guides is designed for use with thirteen- to eighteen-year-olds. *A Life that Counts* will help your group explore some key issues and apply their faith to their daily experiences.

What teenager has never wondered how far is okay when it comes to sex? Or perhaps stumbled on pornography while surfing the web? Or how many young people have asked again and again for guidance from God and wished they understood more about how Christ guides his followers? And what about the daily slog – when boredom sets in, when you return from the big summer festival and hit the ground with a bump. How can you keep a vibrant faith then? This collection of meeting guides tackles all these things and more – what about debt? How can I be a creative Christian? What's marriage about? These 10 sessions, covering a cross-section of issues, are all geared at helping your group with their journey with Christ and inspiring them to develop their spiritual life.

Each meeting plan is ready-to-use in the sense that little additional work or preparation is required. However, you alone will know the particular interests, likes and dislikes of your group and in order to get the most from each session you should spend a few moments reading it first. This will allow you to familiarise yourself with the material, gather any props or equipment which may be required and tweak the outline in order to reflect where your group are at spiritually.

Each session has been tried and tested. All have appeared in *Youthwork* magazine and were devised and put together by Youth workers and specialists. Every session has a worksheet to accompany it, which can be printed from the CD Rom.

Steve Adams
Editor

CONTRIBUTING AUTHORS

Chris Curtis has been involved in youth ministry, with a focus on unchurched young people for the past decade. He currently heads up the Luton Churches Education Trust.

John Allan has had wide experience of youth work and ministry and currently operates from Belmont Chapel, Exeter. He has written on a wide variety of youth-related subjects and is a prolific curriculum writer. He contributes regularly to *Youthwork* magazine.

Steve Adams has written youth curriculum, features and analysis on a variety of subjects and is author of *Music to Move the Soul* and *The Word through Sound* – both youth curriculum books using contemporary music (published by Authentic Media). He is a regular contributor to *Youthwork* magazine and works for Tearfund as part of their editorial team.

MEETING GUIDE:

After the Big Event

Author: John Allan

MEETING AIM: Soul Survivor, Greenbelt, Spring Harvest . . . Teenagers often come back from major Christian events with a new excitement and sense of dedication – which then fizzles away gradually as the glow disappears. This meeting is about understanding the process and keeping the glow. Consequently, it works best with a more committed group (although you could use it with other kids, to help explain why Christians can be genuinely touched by God yet suddenly seem to lose their enthusiasm).

You could use it before going to an event – as preparation and warning – or afterwards to help them reflect on their experience.

CLOTHES SWAP

Send someone out of the room, then get two people to swap (visible!) items of clothing. Call the volunteer back and challenge them to identify what's changed. Do this with three or four people; award a small prize to those who get it right first time.

7 minutes

Say that this game sounds easy, but it can be difficult remembering exactly how things were. We have pictures in our mind which may or may not be true! And when you go to a big event, it leaves a rosy glow behind – 'we had such a great time' – which may or may not correspond to reality. Result: people can be disillusioned and the real experience can be lost.

Ask for memories of the last big event you attended. How did it help people? Did they expect more afterwards than actually happened? Were they upset when others didn't understand their excitement? Did anybody feel they'd simple been conned or hyped? Did anybody feel their life was changed forever? Share your own past experiences too.

1

Say that today we investigate how to benefit most from the big event. Sometimes God does major stuff in our lives, which then goes wrong for several reasons. That happened in the Old Testament too . . .

STILL SMALL VOICE

Briefly outline the story of Elijah (1 Kgs. 18–19): his 'big event' moment on Mount Carmel, where God visibly and powerfully worked through him, followed by sudden decline: running away from Jezebel and nursing a sense of grievance. Say that Elijah was one of only three Bible figures (also Jonah and Moses) who lost the will to live – and all were great heroes for God!

13 minutes

Obviously even those whom God has met with powerfully can lose the plot . . .

Divide into four small groups to study different parts of the story. (If you don't have many kids, summarise the conclusions of two sections, and let them work together on the remaining two.) If your group aren't good at looking up Bible passages, print them out beforehand.

GROUP 1: Why did Elijah run (1 Kgs. 17:2,3; 17:9; 17:20; 18:36–38; 19:2–3)? (Burn out, too many exciting, draining experiences; sudden opposition; realization that life wasn't going to be easier after all.)

GROUP 2: How was he feeling (19:4, 19:10, 19:14)? (Self-pitying; isolated; threatened. He obviously felt God didn't understand the situation. And he'd been overambitious – verse 4.)

GROUP 3: What did God do before speaking to him again (19:5–9, 11–13)? (Restored him physically – food, rest, exercise! You can't burn the candle at both ends without suffering spiritually. Then showed him that 'big events' aren't always where God is – wind, earthquake, fire – we need to learn to hear the gentle whisper too.)

GROUP 4: When God spoke to him, how did that change things (19: 15–18)? (It gave him a concrete plan of action; shared the strain with others; showed him that God had more resources than he imagined – it didn't all depend on him.)

Let each group report back, add extra points as necessary, and ask how does this apply to our 'big event' experiences today? Stress that your emotions and your health affect your spirit. Often mountain-top experiences are followed by deep valleys just because we're tired out.

YOU HAD TO BE THERE

Ask if anybody has come back from a 'big event' and been frustrated because parents, church leaders, or other group members just haven't seemed excited about it? Share any experiences – then tell them half a story: 'A man with an expensive car is pushing it – not driving it – round in circles. He pushes it up to a posh hotel and stays there for a few minutes, paying lots of money to do so. Then he's off again. Put your hand up if you know what he's doing?' Some will get it immediately (he's playing Monopoly); others will be stumped. Let them ask questions and see how long it takes before everybody works it out . . .

Say that puzzled some people because they had the wrong picture in mind. If they'd seen the man, it would have been obvious! Sometimes when you aren't there, you develop a wrong picture. We may come back from a big event with glowing emotions which people at home don't share: they weren't there. The devil can use that to exploit gaps between us and build frustration.

ONE STEP AT A TIME

Now send three people on an obstacle course across the room – litter furniture in their path, get them to hold one hand outstretched, and place a paper cup full of water on their upturned palm. See who can get to the other side first without spillage . . . Run the game a couple of times.

Say: the more you play that game, the more you realize: victory comes to those who don't rush! It's important to concentrate on the next step, and take it slowly. It's the same in Christian living. No one experience, however brilliant, takes you all the way to the finishing post! Indeed, sometimes big experiences actually create new problems!

Remind them of some biblical 'big events' – Moses' burning bush experience (Exodus 3), Gideon's angel experience (Judges 6), Isaiah's temple experience (Isaiah 6) – and ask: what followed these 'big events'? (If they don't know, tell them – the opposition of Pharaoh, the plagues and the desert; the war against a much bigger army with desperately few soldiers; the unpleasant commission of Isaiah 6:9–13.)

Talk about how experiences of God in your own life have taken you one step further, but not solved everything in one go!

EVALUATE

Hand out the worksheet and give them 10 minutes to answer the questions on their own and look at one of the case studies (they will need Bibles for this). If you are looking ahead to when you will be part of a big event, change the questions on the sheet to reflect this.

When everyone's done it, come back together and invite people to feed back what they wrote.

CRISIS, PROCESS OR ABSCESS

George Verwer (the founder of the international mission organisation Operation Mobilisation) often says 'A crisis not followed by a process soon becomes an abscess.' God gives gifts, experiences and thrills to be used as launching-pads – not monuments! To make the best of the big event, we need to come home determined to do something with what we've got. (Ask them what happened to manna when you kept it in a jar? Exod. 16:19–20. You can't live on past blessings.)

Get into small groups. If your group has just been to a big event, discuss together

(a) what you each gained from it

(b) how it could go wrong

(c) what action you need to take to keep the blessing.

If your group is soon to go to an event, discuss

(a) what you hope to get from it

(b) how that might happen

(c) what action you need to take to keep the blessing.

If nothing is recent or immediately scheduled, tell them a story about someone you know who had an unsatisfactory 'big event' experience and discuss: what action should have been taken? Why did the crisis produce the abscess?

Share results and pray together about your conclusions. Ask God to meet with you in the earthquake, wind and fire – but also daily in his gentle whisper.

MEETING GUIDE:

Boredom

Author: John Allan

MEETING AIM: 'It's boring' is one of the biggest teenage objections to practically anything. Why do people get bored? What can we do about it? What has this to do with finding God's purpose and satisfaction in life? These are the kinds of questions this meeting explores. Make sure the meeting itself isn't boring! The subject matter is fairly thoughtful, philosophical and introspective. You may wish to break it up with the odd silly game, just for light relief.

TONIGHT'S SPECIAL GUEST

Beforehand, hang several posters on the wall – some bright and attractive, others dull and predictable. Introduce a special 'guest speaker' whom you have asked to take tonight's meeting. She or he will speak for 40 minutes, after which there will be questions. The 'guest'

12 minutes

is a friend (preferably not well known to the group) who aims to be as boring as possible (potential subjects: 'My Holiday Slides'; 'The Eschatology of Leviticus' etc). His or her style should be dry, repetitive and stumbling, without making it too obvious. Watch how young people react – note down visual signs of boredom and distracted behaviour.

When everything is quietly falling asleep, suddenly another leader rushes into the room. The leader does five unexpected, unusual things, then rushes out again. When the uproar subsides, ask people to go into small groups and write:

– How they felt before it happened;

– What happened, step by step;

– What the interrupting leader was wearing.

Usually descriptions will be pretty inaccurate. Point out that this is what happens when boredom sets in – we fall asleep and stop noticing things. Ask what was it that had made you bored? How could you tell people were bored – how did they react? Share the observations you made of their behaviour, and ask the 'guest speaker' how she or he set about making the talk so boring.

Say that today we investigate boredom. First: what is it?

WHAT'S BOREDOM, AND WHO CARES?

Back in small groups, discuss these questions:

- How do you feel when you're bored?
- What gets you bored most often?
- What are you thinking when you're bored?
- Which posters on the wall are most boring?

Share ideas. Say that teenagers probably get more bored than anybody else. Reason: you're at an age when your personal abilities are developed and very new – you want to use them to the max and experience everything. Frustration sets in when you can't do something decisive. And teenagers appreciate excitement more than any other age group; we want things to happen right now. (Perhaps talk about Rehoboam, or the young Moses, and how youthful impatience can lead to bad decisions.)

Young people often think the church is the most boring institution in history. Does God want us to be bored?

GOD – CHAIRMAN OF THE BORED?

Either in small groups, or all together, do some Bible study and investigate these questions:

- What does God want life on this planet to be like? (Ps 104:10–24)
- What does God want your individual life to be like? (Ps 103:2–12)
- What do Christians have that non-Christians don't, which can prevent boredom? (Col 3:1–4, 23–24)

Compare answers. Sum up by saying our creative, exciting God wants life to be colourful, has a plan for our lives, and gives us real purpose when we follow him.

LET'S BE REALLY BORING

Ask each small group to write a story, compose a song, deliver a talk, draw a picture, or prepare a sketch, in as boring a way as possible. (They could draw cards out of a hat to decide which type of activity they are assigned. Then either give them a subject, or let them draw cards for it.) After five or six minutes, bore one another to death with the results.

13 minutes

Ask them why were these things so boring. What was especially mind-numbingly awful?

Sum up by saying we get bored when things don't: seem to involve us personally in any way; look attractive (remind them of the posters); appeal to interests we already have; appear understandable.

Read the following text (used in a psychological experiment in America) and see what they can remember of it:

PSYCHOLOGICAL EXPERIMENT

The procedure is actually quite simple. First you arrange things into different groups. Of course, one pile may be sufficient depending on how much there is to do . . . After the procedure is completed, one arranges the materials into different groups again, Then they can be put into their proper places. Eventually they will be used once more and the whole cycle will then have to be repeated.

Then tell them what it's about – sorting laundry – and read it again. Ask: did it make any more sense this time? Was it more interesting? Of course – because you knew what it was about. Say: now that we understand why we get bored, maybe we can find ways of dealing with it.

APATHY ATTACK

Get the groups to take on one (or more) of these case studies each:

10 minutes

Case 1: Tim has to revise a year's course material in sociology for his exams. He couldn't stand it the first time round, and the thought of spending weeks revising fills him with dread. How can he get down to it?

Case 2: Amanda goes to the most boring church service in the history of the world – because her parents want her to. She longs to worship God in her own way, but the staid prayers, long silences and six-verse hymns do nothing for her.

Case 3: Mark is in a really dead-end job, flipping burgers and earning very little. Yet right now he has no other options, and he really needs the money. From boredom, many employees don't do the job as they're supposed to, but as a Christian, he feels that's not right. Still, he has no enthusiasm for it, and hates going to work.

Case 4: Sally has a friend who really needs to get a life. She never wants to do anything interesting, looks drab and dreadful, and makes the most boring conversation. Sally feels she should stick with this girl because she has no other friends, but she's being driven crazy.

Case 5: Darren is on holiday with his grandparents and having a dreadful time. It would help if it stopped raining, but even so, they aren't doing much. His grandparents are very kind but they don't have much energy, only ever seem to visit garden centres, and don't want him to go out without them.

Compare results. From the ensuing discussion, make a flipchart or OHP list of good strategies for dealing with boredom. Say: let's remember some of these ideas – you never know when you'll need them.

THE GIFT OF BOREDOM

Make the point that boredom isn't always bad. God sometimes puts people into frustrating situations so that they will change their thinking, develop a burning

15 minutes

ambition, or deepen their commitment. Hand out the worksheets and ask them to get into pairs and spend 10 minutes considering the people in the section entitled: 'Useful Boredom'.

When they have done this, allow time for feedback. Then make the point that when our life circumstances aren't brilliant, we shouldn't blame God but ask 'is there a purpose in this? Has God made me bored for a good reason?' Allow them some further time to complete the section marked Art of Boredom.

WRAP UP

Pray together, thanking God that He is the creator of excitement, colour and variety. Ask him to forgive you when you miss his purpose and become bored with life unnecessarily. But ask for patience in situations where he's deliberately frustrating you in order to teach something new. And thank him that he has a purpose for your life, and wants to fill it with joy, satisfaction and thrills.

MEETING GUIDE:

The Beauty of Original Thinking

Author: John Allan

MEETING AIM: To explore the meaning of creativity, examine how God built it in to human life and encourage the growth of it in the life of your group or church.

PREPARATION: Drop a blob of ink on to absorbent paper, folding it in half, and opening it out to create a 'mirror image' picture. Photocopy it four or five times. Get a video clip of a football match, showing somebody (perhaps Ginola, Owen or Giggs) doing something inspired and unexpected. Bring along a CD track with an arresting musical arrangement.

Get a copy of *Dead Poets' Society* and wind it to the point where Robin Williams makes his schoolboys climb on the desk to see life from a different angle. Place in a hat a number of cards, each bearing the name of a household object ('a hammer', 'a screwdriver', 'a frying pan', etc.). Cut out examples of some great advertisements and some poor uninspired ones from the newspaper.

OUTSIDE THE BOX

Give out copies of the worksheet and tell the group to look at the Circle Puzzle section. Ask if anyone can draw four lines, passing through each circle just once, without taking the pen off the paper. Most will fail! The answer is like this:

10 minutes

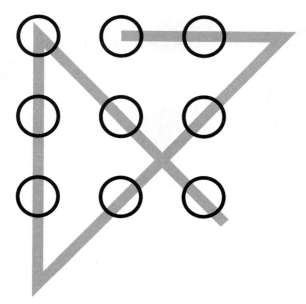

Ask them why they couldn't see the answer. Most people are mesmerized by the 'box' shape and assume you must draw all the lines inside the box. But for real results, you need to go outside, and see possibilities which most people miss.

Creativity is the power to see 'outside the box' and glimpse things that others miss. That's how Columbus discovered America (imagining the world as round, not flat). That's how Edison discovered the gramophone (imagining sounds being stored in plastic).

Divide into small groups. Give out copies of the inkblot picture; ask each group to think up a creative title for it. Give a small prize to the most inventive one. Say that creativity isn't just wild imagination – but original thinking with the power to explain things, and bring ideas together in a new way.

THE GREATER CREATOR

Hand out Bibles and get the group to look at the second section of their worksheet entitled 'Creative Creator'. Staying in their small groups ask them to spend some time working through the Bible passages and questions.

15 minutes

When everyone has finished compare results. Say that creativity is part of the nature of all humans, not just artists and sculptors.

Show the football video clip and ask who was creative here?
– What did he do?
– What might somebody less brilliant have done?
– What would have been the obvious thing to do?

Play the CD and ask what's creative about this? Get different groups to listen to different instruments and note how, for example, the drums add flourishes and change rhythm occasionally, or the bass line suddenly changes. Say that this is creativity – doing the unexpected, introducing variety and new perspectives.

Play the *Dead Poets' Society* clip. Ask: what is he trying to do? Why? Can something so simple really change people?

Now ask each mini-group to share with each other 'my most creative moment this week'. Get them to pick the best story to tell the whole group. Award a prize for the one voted most inspired.

Finally, ask the group what does 'uncreativity' look like? What's the difference between creative and uncreative praying? Worship? Evangelism? (If time allows, work out together a running order for the most uncreative church service they can think of . . .)

YOU'RE AN ELEPHANT

What does creativity include? Adam named the animals; dividing things up, imposing patterns and connecting ideas, is all part of being creative. Produce the hat and get each mini-group to draw out three cards each. Say that you have to think of an original team game for the youth group, using these objects as part of the equipment. What could you do? After a few minutes, check results and award prizes.

8 minutes

Look at Acts 19:8–10, Mark 3:8–10, 2 Samuel 12:1–7. What's creative in these stories?

THE GOOD, THE BAD AND THE BORING

Circulate the newspaper ads around the groups, allowing a minute for them to look at each before handing it on. Ask them to mark each out of ten for creativity. Discuss results.

Ask: why were some so much better than others? What makes us see some things as clever, beautiful or attractive?

Say: creativity is about taking the trouble to do things well. It's about variety, colour, life and surprises. Ask: how much creativity would outsiders find in the life of our group? In the style of our church?

LET'S GET CREATIVE

Sum up some principles we've established so far.

1. Creativity is about original thinking.
2. Creativity is about variety and contrast.
3. Creativity is about bringing unlikely ideas together.
4. Creativity is about beauty and attractiveness.

Say: now let's exercise our creativity. We're going to 'brainstorm'. Explain the rules: the aim is to generate as many ideas as possible in a short space of time, just shouting them out and writing them down. It doesn't matter if they're crazy. Nobody is allowed to say 'That's impossible' or 'That's stupid'. After three minutes, you will stop and look at the list together, and decide which would work. Usually, the freedom to be totally creative, and not have to think practically, throws up a few ideas which look daft to start with, but actually contain the germ of ideas you'd never have thought of otherwise.

The subject for your 'brainstorm' can be whatever you like – ideally something related to your own group situation such as: How can we make our next youth service really different? How can we plan a unique, arresting event to bring friends along to? How can we make our prayer times really exciting? What can we do at our next weekend away that we've never done before?

After this exercise, say: creativity is one of God's most special gifts. He values human imagination and originality (Ex. 31:1–6), and depends on us to express his exciting, unique, attractive character to the world by being exciting, unique and attractive ourselves. End by praying that God will make you more and more creative, in every area of your life together.

MEETING GUIDE:

Debt

Author: John Allan

MEETING AIM: A recent YMCA survey shows that 90 per cent of their young residents believe that it is very important to avoid debt – but 50 per cent are currently in debt. 90 per cent think they should have a pension; only 10 per cent do.

Part of Christian discipleship is good stewardship, which includes knowing how to cope with money. Yet all too often young people receive little help with this – although they are the prime targets for advertisers, manufacturers and entertainment providers. This meeting should help your group think through their habits and priorities. You might want to obtain a copy of the YMCA survey 'More Than Just A PIN Number' by calling 020 8509 4557, or going to http://www.npi.org.uk . If you have a friend or church member with professional financial skills, perhaps you could invite them to attend as a consultant and expert witness . . .

Watch carefully the comments individuals make in the discussion times. Some of your group may reveal dangerously immature attitudes to money, possessions and debt, and you might want to have a personal chat with them later.

INTRODUCTION

Divide into four small groups. One representative of each group plays 'Backwards Monopoly' while everyone else watches. The only differences from real Monopoly are: you have to buy whatever property you land on; you can borrow money from any other player you like, and they can't refuse, but the sum owed doubles every time you throw the dice thereafter; if you go bankrupt, you keep playing, but your debt doubles every time you throw the dice; the game ends after five minutes exactly; and the winner is the person with the most horrendous debts.

8 minutes

OWING TO?

Say: that was just for fun – but it shows how owing money can quickly become a difficult problem! Debt is one of the biggest unacknowledged problems for young people in the world today. In this session, we do some thinking about it.

7 minutes

Hand out the worksheets and give the young people a few minutes to look at the questions under the section 'Why Debt?'

Come back together and compare results. Then say 'now let's look at what God has to say about it . . .'

MONEY MONEY MONEY

Give each group a list of these verses: Habakkuk 2:7, Luke 19:23, Exodus 22:25, Nehemiah 5:9–11, Deuteronomy 15:1 and this list of questions:

10 minutes

Which verse says that . . .

- it's all right to lend money, but wrong to make extortionate rates of interest?

- Jesus didn't disapprove of investing money to gain interest on it?

- people who try to make unjust profits will ultimately be destroyed?

- Old Testament Israelites were forbidden to charge each other interest at all?

- debts had to be forgiven after a certain length of time?

Check results. Ask the group what guidelines might this give us for our financial dealings today? God says much more to lenders than to borrowers – what does this suggest? Does it mean there aren't any rules for borrowers? – can we do what we like?

Say that the reason that God is so strongly against debt is because it destroys the potential of our lives. Let's look at how it works.

TIED HAND AND FOOT

10 minutes

Each group takes a pack of cards, shuffles and deals the same number to each member. Everyone in turn then puts a card, face up, on a pile in the middle, until their cards are exhausted; then the pack is shuffled and dealt out again. Do this three times. Whenever anyone turns up an ace, the others take a piece of string and tie it between two parts of his body (e.g. wrist to ankle, neck to knee). After the three rounds, line up the entire group and make them run a race for a chocolate bar at the other end of the room.

After all the groups have raced, say that none of these races was fair – because everyone was tied up differently. And their handicaps came quite randomly; poor skills or bad judgement weren't really involved. That's a picture of what debt can do: it makes life unfair; we become hamstrung and hindered from living as God wants us to. Write these words on an OHP or flip-chart one by one, and ask the group how might debt produce each of these results. What else might it do?

Depression • Self-disgust • Frustration and rage
Fear • Guilt • Boredom • Apathy

(Alternatively, give each group one of the words, and ask them to create a short sketch showing how debt might produce this emotion. If you have time, talk about what this can mean internationally, and why Christians are so concerned about Two-Thirds World debt – perhaps using materials from the Jubilee Campaign or from http://www.oneworld.org)

It sounds as if we need to plan our finances carefully. But what does God think about planning? Let's do a memory test.

NO PLANS, PLEASE, WE'RE SPIRITUAL

10 minutes

Read out three passages one after another: Matthew 6:25–7, Proverbs 31:10–20, Ecclesiastes 11:1–6.

Then get the groups to sort out which statements are TRUE and which FALSE. (If more physical activity is needed, make one corner of the room 'true' and the other 'false'; read each statement in turn, and give people ten seconds to dash to the corner they think is correct.)

- Jesus said we shouldn't plan for the future.
- Jesus said we shouldn't worry about the future.
- The good wife didn't concern herself with money.
- Ecclesiastes says we shouldn't be idle.
- Ecclesiastes says we should try different ways to succeed and not put all our eggs in one basket.
- The good wife is a good trader.
- The good wife works hard for herself and her family, and ignores everybody else.

Review the correct answers and point out what they teach about our attitude to prosperity, planning, and care for those poorer than us.

HOW TO BE RICH

Turn to the second part of the worksheets – the section marked 'Managing Money'. Ask: so what's the best way of looking after our money, paying our debts and achieving prosperity? Allow five minutes for them to complete the 'Money, Money, Money' quiz then get feedback as to which methods people thought were safe or dangerous, and why.

WRAP UP

Review everything you've covered in this session. If you have an 'expert witness' present, let your 'witness' make a final comment. Then pray together for those you know who have real money problems; for those living in countries crippled by debt; and for yourselves, that God will give you the wisdom, self-discipline and foresight to be good stewards of what he's committed to you, and to use your goods to help those who can't help themselves.

MEETING GUIDE:

Escaping Reality?

Author: John Allan

MEETING AIM: This session will look at the amount of time society spends engaged in fictional activities (TV soaps, films, computer games etc). It will help young people assess their own lives, look at whether unreality is a big part, and ask how this influences their lives. Young Christians all too often have their minds shaped by the same myths and fantasies that dominate the culture around us: this is a gentle attempt to prick some bubbles and induce realistic thinking. The outline probably works better with committed Christians of over fourteen, but can be adapted for others.

PREPARATION: Write on five scraps of paper: 'Proverbs 10:23', 'Proverbs 12:9', 'Proverbs 14:23', 'Ecclesiastes 3:9–13', 'Psalm 14:1'. Insert each scrap into a balloon, then blow the balloons up. Get hold of video clips, or publicity materials, for the films mentioned below (or others like them). Hint: you can find clips of the newer ones on the films' Internet sites.

WHERE AM I REALLY?

Blu-tack a small prize to the ceiling. Take four volunteers and give each three markers (small circles of paper will do). Blindfold them and spin them round three times. Then allow them to walk around the room (watch they don't hurt themselves) and drop their markers when they

12 minutes

think they're directly under the prize. They have three attempts. Finally, give the prize to the one who comes closest.

Say that when you've lost your bearings, it's difficult to know where you really are. You may be convinced you're in one place – and yet be somewhere totally different. But you can't live life properly unless you have some sense of reality.

Give everyone a piece of paper and a pen. Ask them to write down:

1. How many hours they have spent this week watching fictional TV programmes (i.e. anything telling a made-up story)?

2. How many hours watching videos or films in the last fortnight?

3. How many hours reading fictional books or magazines?

4. How many hours playing computer games, Nintendo or arcade games?

Work out a group total of hours spent in these activities. What percentage is this of the time we actually spend awake? (Probably 224 hours a fortnight.) Make the point that a huge and growing slice of people's lives is spent on fantasy activities; it's been said that our society has a 'fiction addiction'. Today we're going to explore what all this is doing to us.

LIFE IS A MOVIE

Show publicity for, or play clips from, one of the *Harry Potter* films, *The Lord of the Rings* films, *The Truman Show* and *The Matrix*. Discuss what explains the massive popularity of such films. Partly it's our urge to escape into a different world in which there are new possibilities, simpler relationships, exciting powers. Or our fascination with seeing ordinary life in a radically different way from our normal perspective.

Ask: what dangers might there be in spending too much of your time in fantasy?

ONE FOOT IN REALITY

Collect answers, but don't discuss. Instead, ask five volunteers to play a simple game. They must fold their arms, lift one leg off the ground, and try to knock each other over. Before they start, ask the others to write down who they think will win. Play, and see if they were right.

Now play again – but this time one player is allowed to keep both feet on the floor. She or he will almost certainly win, and almost everyone will be found to have voted for them. Ask why. Then talk about the fact that it's because someone with both feet on the ground will always be more secure than someone with only one foot in reality. Make the point: it's easy to move on from consuming other people's fictions, to constructing fantasy ideas about our own lives – which don't actually help us face reality, but just detach us from it.

ANY DREAM WILL DO

Ask: what fantasies do people often spin about their romantic lives? (Examples: 'Some day he will come back to me', 'I'm too ugly ever to get a girlfriend', 'If I sleep with him/spend money on him/buy trendy clothes, he will love me'). Put them into small groups and ask each

to come up with the 'Top five fantasies' which people kid themselves into believing, in these categories (one per group): family life (e.g.: 'the trouble with our family is my brother') the future of the planet (e.g.: 'if we all work together, peace will come') my career (e.g.: 'some day I'll be a star and my problems will be over') what God's really like (e.g.: 'God is always sitting there judging me and waiting for me to slip')

Compare results.

LIVING IN DREAMLAND

Now give each group the 'top five' list of a different group. Ask them to look at these ideas, and use them to explore two questions:

(a) What factors make people attracted to these fantasies (e.g. wish-fulfilment, compensation, unwillingness to face facts)?

(b) Is fantasy always bad for us or does it have any use in our lives?

Compare answers. Say: perhaps it's because our society faces bigger questions than any before, and more terrifying possibilities, that we take so much refuge in fiction. We have so much freedom to shape our own lives that we find it hard to handle.

FICTION ADDICTION?

Hand out the worksheet and allow seven minutes for them to fill it in – it is fairly self-explanatory. When they have done this, come back together and ask if anyone is brave enough to share their answers. Refer back to these at the end when the group prays for each other.

10 minutes

HELLO, THIS IS PLANET EARTH CALLING

The Bible is keen that we should burst our bubbles and see reality clearly. Produce the balloons with Bible verses inside. Throw them out into the group and get people to pop each in turn, reading what's inside. Get them to look up each verse and discuss: which of our fantasy balloons does it try to pop? What does it say about living in reality?

10 minutes

WAKE UP AND SMELL THE COFFEE

Say: one man always saw things accurately – Jesus. And sometimes the way he saw things stunned others, because it was such a different 'take' on reality.

15 minutes

Bible study. In small groups, look at one of these passages each:

John 9:1–7; Luke 18:9–14; Matthew 9:9–13; Mark 7:14–23; Luke 21:1–4

After five minutes, ask the whole group:

(a) In our passage, what was different about Jesus' viewpoint from anybody else's?

(b) Why was his viewpoint closer to reality?

(c) What does that tell us about living today?

Finally, read together 1 Thessalonians 5:5–11. Take a few minutes to think about the implications of 'belonging to the day'. Ask people to think silently about the difficult realities they might be running away from; the fantasies they are tempted to believe about themselves; the easy excuses we find for not living in the way we know we should.

End with group prayer referring back to the things young people wrote on their worksheets.

MEETING GUIDE:

Guidance

Author: John Allan

MEETING AIM: To answer the question: how do we work out God's will for our lives?

PREPARATION: Print out a picture with lots of detail in it (a street scene, maybe, or a picture of a crowded room). But insert a small white square somewhere in it so that a tiny part of the picture is omitted.

Think about your own experiences of God's guidance, and be prepared to share some stories. This will help the abstract principles come to life for them in an understandable way.

Plan the introductory 'treasure hunt' carefully, so that nobody can get lost en route, and put up all the signs just before they're needed.

Make four sets of 'Circumstances' cards and one set of 'Great Advice' cards (described below).

INTRODUCTION

Before they arrive, put a notice on the door of your normal meeting room saying that the venue has changed, and asking them to go somewhere else (location A) for further instructions. When they get to location A, they should find another notice referring them to location B . . . where they find a message telling them to ring your mobile number. As each of them rings, tell them they've been tricked. They should come to the normal place anyway.

5 minutes

When they've all arrived, say: that was just an introduction to today's topic. To find what you wanted, you had to follow a set of instructions, one step at a time; and up to the last step you didn't now what the end was going to be. Life is often like that. God promises to guide us. But he does it one step at a time, and sometimes we're surprised to find out where we end up!

So how does he guide us? When do we know it's really a message from him?

STARING YOU IN THE FACE

Show them, for 10 seconds, the picture with the white square missing. Then cover it up and ask, 'What did you notice about that picture?'

Most people will immediately say, 'there was a bit missing'. If you question them about the picture's details, you'll find they noticed what wasn't there, much more than what was!

Say: sometimes we get worried about understanding God's will. We're scared we'll miss it. But we need to remember that 99 per cent of it is already clear to us – it's there in the Bible. Give out the worksheets and invite them to look at the illustration under the section headed 'Getting Guidance'. Explain that they should fill in as many blanks as they can for each section. Under the section 'Ways God has already guided us', they should write things such as 'The Bible', 'Wisdom of church leaders' and 'conscience'. Under the heading 'Ways God gives direct guidance to people', they should write things such as 'prophetic words', 'dreams' and 'divine appointments'.

When the group have filled in this section make the point that God's already told us how he wants us to behave and how we should treat others. As with the 99 per cent of the illustration most of our time should be spent living out this guidance which he's given us in the Bible. Only a small percentage of the time does God guide through words and divine appointments and we must not spend too much time focusing on these.

Say: today we investigate four of God's key methods . . .

NARROWING IT DOWN

First, God guides us through circumstances. Give an illustration of this from your own experience. Divide into four groups. Give each a set of 'circumstances' cards and say: imagine you need guidance. Should you go on the youth weekend next month, or stay and help your Dad fix his car? (Each of the cards should contain one of the 'circumstances' that might be important in making your decision and one card should be left blank.)

'You can't really afford the weekend unless you earn some money quickly'

'Your Dad really needs your help and is counting on it'

'The youth leader has just phoned up and asked you personally to go'

'Your sleeping bag needs replacing'

Ask each group to decide which of these circumstances they would think is most important in making your decision. How would they rate them in order? None of them are absolutely conclusive, though. Can they think of something that might happen – a circumstance God might send along – which would make his will clear and unmistakable? Ask them to write it on the blank card. Then check conclusions.

BIBLE STUFF

Sometimes God uses good advisers to help us find his will. Say: the Bible is full of stories about advice that changed somebody's life. Give each group a 'Great Advice' card. (Each card should contain a situation, and Bible references, as follows):

1) The problem: Moses was wearing himself out by trying to sort out all the Israelites' problems single-handedly.

      The adviser: Jethro his father-in-law

      The advice: Ex 18:14–24

2) The problem: Naaman was told to bathe in the river Jordan to cure his skin disease, but felt he was being ridiculed.

> The advisers: Naaman's soldiers
>
> The advice: 2 Kings 5:11–14

3) The problem: David was on the point of rashly destroying Abigail's husband, who had offended him badly.

> The adviser: Abigail
>
> The advice: 1 Samuel 32–35

4) The problem: Mordecai had just uncovered a plot to exterminate the Jews, but Esther was unsure about confronting the King with the evidence.

> The adviser: Mordecai
>
> The advice: Esther 4:5–16

Ask each group to look at 'their' situation, read the Bible verses, and then fill in their answers to the three questions on the work sheet.

Check each group's results. Summarise: often God's wisdom comes to us through others. We need to be listening for his voice behind the comments of those we know and trust.

MISUSING THE BIBLE

Say that a third way in which God guides us is through Scripture. But we need to read it in context! We can't make any passage mean whatever we want it to.

Let them try it. Draw their attention to the section on the work sheet marked 'Pot-Luck Guidance'. Explain that they have to try and solve each of the problems listed on the worksheet by opening the Bible at random, and 'applying' the first verse they put their finger on. If the verse selected is irrelevant, they can try again – to a maximum of three times. They should fill in the section on the worksheet.

Give them five minutes to do this then check results together. It's uncanny how often they'll find something which (with imagination) can be stretched to fit! As they call theirs out explain and discuss how this distorts the real point of those verses.

Tell them the old story about the man who did this and got the verse 'And Judas went and hanged himself.' He tried again – only to get 'Go and do likewise.' And on a third attempt: 'And what you do, do quickly.' It probably never happened – but it might have!

FUNNY FEELINGS

Finally, for a few minutes, play any game you like which requires a referee (table football? table tennis?). After a couple of minutes, the referee should begin making bad decisions, which gradually become more and more outrageous, until the game is in chaos.

10 minutes

Point out: bad referees are no use. Sometimes you make sensible progress only if you trust the ref. Read out Colossians 3:15; literally it means, 'Let the peace of God be referee in your hearts'.

Say: sometimes, even when you've looked at the circumstances, consulted wise friends, and read the Bible carefully, you'll still be in doubt about God's will. In these situations, he may guide you with his peace. You'll feel happy about one of the alternatives, and uneasy about the other. When everything else is finely balanced, God sometimes uses this way of getting through to us.

WRAP UP

Remind them of each of the four methods you've looked at. Encourage them, when stumped to ask: what do the circumstances tell me? What do friends say?

5 minutes

Does Scripture direct me here? And where is God's peace to be found?

Allow five minutes in closing for them to think about a situation they are in for which they need guidance and to write down the answers to the four questions on the worksheet under the section 'Four Questions'. If they don't know the answers to all the questions challenge them to go and find them out this week.

Come back together and pray, thanking God for his willingness to reveal his purposes to us. And ask him to make you increasingly sensitive to what he's saying, for your benefit and his glory too.

MEETING GUIDE:

Internet Porn

Author: John Allan

MEETING AIM: The Internet is a great communications medium – but what is it used for? Between 40 per cent and 80 per cent of Internet traffic – at least 13.4 million gigabytes each month – is pornography. Porn provides $1.9 billion of trade every year, and the figure is growing steadily.

One reason for this boom is that the Internet makes it so easy to find unhealthy material. People who would be embarrassed to buy magazines in a shop can surf freely without detection, and lie easily about their age.

The sheer numbers involved, and the size of the market, are conferring new respectability on pornography, because 'everybody does it'. The hero of the TV series 'God, the Devil and Bob' has a large Internet porn collection. Playboy is respectable again (and is developing a new hardcore dimension to its activities). Porn actresses are treated as superstars. A survey last year among US Christians indicated that 33 per cent of clergy and 36 per cent of laity have visited porn sites.

So, it's vital for Christian young people to understand the dangers, know how to avoid them, and receive help to break free from entanglements they've contracted. The aim of this meeting is to open up discussion on the subject and show why freedom is desirable and possible. It may help your group to reflect on other areas of addictive, compulsive behaviour too.

BEFORE YOU START: On the notice board pin up a sign clearly labelled 'DO NOT LOOK BEHIND HERE'. On the reverse side, write 'WHAT DID I JUST TELL YOU?'

YOU ARE WHAT YOU THINK

Play the old Pip Wilson game 'Knickers'. One person in the middle is asked a barrage of questions by the group, on any subject(s) they like; to every question, the reply must be 'Knickers', said without smiling or laughing. If the person in the middle breaks down, someone else takes their place. The winner is the one who remains poker-faced the longest.

10 minutes

Ask: how do you win this game? Only by keeping your thoughts strictly under control. How do you lose? By letting mental pictures overwhelm your imagination. Our minds are funny things; if thoughts gain control of us, they can dominate our behaviour, however much we struggle.

Read Proverbs 4:23–25. Introduce the subject of Internet porn (perhaps by quoting figures above). Say: this is a staggeringly successful new route for evil to make inroads into people's thought-lives today. We need to know about it and understand why it's dangerous.

Point to the sign on the notice board, and ask: how many people know what it says on the other side? Many of us couldn't resist having a look. Others may have obeyed, but we all felt a burning curiosity about it. Why? Because when something's off limits – yet enticingly available – it becomes irresistibly attractive. That's the temptation of porn: we may not be demented perverts, but we think, 'It can't harm just to have a peep . . .'

PORN EXPERT

Test their impressions with a true-or-false quiz:

10 minutes

Internet porn is . . .

1. Controlled by a few shadowy multi-millionaire vice kings. *(False: e-commerce makes it possible for thousands of small-time suppliers to set up their own 'cottage industry', and thousands of outlets are opening every day.)*
2. Worth as much annually as all rock music and country music record sales in America, and more than the total revenue from airline tickets. *(True)*

3. Difficult to track down unless you know what you're looking for. *(False: porn sites constantly crop up in search engine results, send out 'spam' e-mails, and disguise themselves as something they're not in order to draw people in.)*

4. A male problem; women aren't attracted. *(False: there has been a dramatic surge in female involvement, although many women prefer fantasy 'virtual sex' with strangers in chat-rooms, to collecting pictures and movies.)*

5. Something that hurts only the person who uses it. *(False: families, especially wives, are damaged, see www.estheronline.org)*

MIND YOUR MIND

Say that we need to find out what God thinks about all this. Porn isn't addressed in Scripture (apart from wealthy Roman emperors, nobody in those days had a collection) but some key principles are. In small groups, look at these verses and discuss the following questions. How do they apply to the subject we're discussing? Do they affect our attitude to Internet porn?

Philippians 4:8 *(answer: this tells us what we should fill our thoughts with)*

Job 31:1 *(our attitude to the opposite sex)*

Ephesians 5:3–4 *(the character we should have)*

2 Timothy 2:3–6 *(the use of our time and money)*

Matthew 5:27–8 *(sexual misbehaviour starts with our thoughts)*

Sum up by saying that our sexual drive is incredibly powerful, and if it isn't kept in the correct place, it can dominate our life, distort our perspectives and frustrate all that God wants to do with us. Read 1 Thessalonians 4:3–5.

START WITH THE THOUGHTS

Hand out copies of the worksheet. Allow a few minutes for them to read the instructions and fill in the sheet. Then have a few minutes silence during which you encourage them to offer their minds to God for him to renew, and listen to what God wants them to fill their

renewed minds with. Encourage them to write into the spaces in the diagram (next to their previous six things) any new things God shows them.

I'M A BIT TANGLED UP JUST NOW

Divide into groups of five or six; each group forms a circle, with everyone facing inwards, both hands thrust outwards. Everyone grasps two other hands (at random) across the circle. Then, without breaking contact, try to untie the knot so that people are standing in a straight line holding hands.

Some groups may manage it. Most will end up becoming more and more knotted and confused. Sometimes it looks as if the knot is coming out – then it snarls up again. Say that this illustrates the problem with porn. It ties you up in knots, and the more you try, the more involved you become. You start by thinking, 'I can break away any time I like' – but you become progressively entangled.

Ask them how does this entanglement start? How many of the group have stumbled across Internet porn unwittingly – or been tricked into finding it?

Steve Lane, former pornography producer, now a Christian, says his colleagues would harvest e-mail addresses from Christian websites, then send them messages containing web links. One click on the unknown link, and the receiver is taken to a porn site. The porn industry strains every nerve to compromise believers. We need to know how to resist!

FIGHTING BACK

So how do we do it? And if someone is already developing a habit of looking occasionally in the wrong places – how do they disentangle themselves? In groups, brainstorm ways of resisting the porn merchants. Compare lists and vote on the best ideas. If these haven't been mentioned, ensure they are included:

(a) Talking to somebody about it is the quickest way of defusing a growing problem. Get help; don't struggle alone.

(b) Making a clean break is vital. Don't try to taper off bit by bit – just stop it. Say no.

(c) Consciously claim God's resources, and submit to his authority, every day (Rom. 6:11–14).

(d) Find other things to engross your mind; don't keep thinking about it.

You'll find other ideas at sites like www.pureintimacy.org

WRAP UP

Spend some time in praying for one another – and for the lonely thousands across the world who have strayed into the grip of something that is blighting and destroying the healthy relationships and clear perspectives they should be enjoying. Pray that the Holy Spirit will give you the power and wisdom to stay well away, and to encourage one another to become so excited about living for God that you don't have room to become obsessed with cheap imitation fulfilment.

Sex, Relationships and Marriage

Author: Steve Adams

MEETING AIM: To look at how young people perceive sex, marriage and relationships, and to help them take the whole area more seriously. This session will help unearth what your group think on these issues. Use what they reveal to spark further discussion.

GROUP REACTIONS

Start the session with a game. Get the group into twos, and stand them with their partners in a line. Tell them you're going to read from a list of different words. They must react, as a pair, to each word by striking one of the following poses and freezing:

7 minutes

HUSH-HUSH: One person cups their hand around the other person's ear and pretends to be whispering to them.

DISDAIN: One of them should point, as if at something in the distance. The other crosses their arms, and both wear strong looks of disdain.

UPSET: One person wipes their eyes as if crying and upset. The other puts a hand on their shoulder offering comfort.

HAPPY: The partners should hug and look as happy as they possibly can.

After you read each word, allow them a minute to confer, then say 'pose'. At that point, the last couple to strike a pose is out. Pick one couple each time and find out why they chose that particular pose. Use these words: Sex; Relationships; Pregnant; Condoms; Marriage; Commitment; Love; Divorce. Be sure to note which poses are used for which words – you'll refer back to them later.

BRAINSTORM

Split the group along gender lines with girls one end and boys the other. You will stand in the centre and ask the questions below. For each question you ask, both teams must field a different player who comes to you in the centre. Ask the question and give each player ten seconds to decide their answer without consulting their team. On your signal, they must shout their answer out. Award a point for each right answer.

■ The legal age for getting married is...?
(Sixteen with parental consent, eighteen without.)

■ True or false: more boys favour lowering the age of marriage than girls. *(True: a quarter of teen boys and a fifth of teen girls want marriage legalised at sixteen without parental consent.)*

■ What did the apostle Paul tell people to do if they were burning with passion? *(Get married: 1 Corinthians 7:9)*

■ What percentage of thirteen to fifteen-year-olds believe it's wrong to have sex outside of marriage: (A) one in three (B) one in seven (C) one in 10
(B – one in seven).

■ In Judges, a dead woman was cut into pieces and sent to each of the 12 tribes after she was attacked and sexually assaulted by evil men. True or false? *(True: Judges 19:29)*

■ The legal age for sexual intercourse is...? *(Sixteen.)*

■ 23 per cent of teenage girls believe divorce is wrong, but only 15 per cent of lads do. True or false? *(False – the percentages are the other way around.)*

■ What percentage of girls have had intercourse by the age of 16: A. 25 per cent B. 35 per cent C. 50 per cent? *(A: 25 per cent.)*

(Source: Key Data on Adolescence 2003)

OAP PERSPECTIVE

Try to organise for a pensioner to visit the group to give some analysis on changes they've seen over their life in terms of sex and relationships in society. Give them five minutes (try to be strict) to talk, with the brief: 'Three ways romantic relationships and sex have changed in society since I was a teenager'.

SEX CULTURE

Building on the talk from your older guest highlight how much, over the past few decades, the approach to sex and relationships has changed: in 1964, 13 per cent of boys and 4 per cent of girls under sixteen had had intercourse. Today this stands at 30 per cent of boys and 25 per cent of girls.

Have a pile of lads' and girls' magazines ready – ask them to bring some of their favourites. Get them to spend five minutes going through counting how many adverts / features / images / photos relate to sex or relationships. Feed back.

Ask what message comes through these images? Suggest that the message being put across is that sex and relationships are a game to enjoy and that marriage, commitment and loyalty are despised and seen as sad or 'grown-up'.

Refer back to the reactions from the 'Group Reactions' quiz at the start to support this. What poses were struck to represent words like sex, marriage and commitment?

Give out the handouts, one per person and get them into pairs. Allow five minutes for them to discuss and fill in the first column: 'Society's Views'.

Tell them you're now going to look at some common issues young people struggle with when dealing with the idea of sex, relationships and marriage.

BIBLE GUIDANCE

Split the group into five smaller teams and give one of the following to each. If the group is a small one, have fewer small groups and share the extra passages around. Explain they are looking at issues which often prove to be barriers to healthy romantic relationships. Give them five minutes to look at the verse(s) and discuss the following questions.

■ AN UNWILLINGNESS TO COMMIT (Gen. 29:15–18)

Jacob works for Laban for seven years to win Rachel's hand in marriage.

- What's the most selfless act you've done to win someone over?
- Does commitment freak you out? Why?

■ AN UNREALISTIC PERCEPTION OF RELATIONSHIPS (Mt. 8:19–20)

A man promises to stick with Jesus without considering the cost.

- Should relationships be costly?
- Would you think about what a relationship might cost you before entering into it?

■ AN ABSENCE OF BALANCE – SWINGING FROM 'DATE AND DUMP' TO 'MARRY OR DUMP' (Jas. 1:5–8)

A call to seek wisdom and avoid being unstable and indecisive.

- Have you swung from hot to cold regarding relationships you've been in?
- Is this normal – what can be done about it?

■ AN INABILITY TO APPROACH THE PHYSICAL SIDE OF RELATIONSHIPS IN A GROWN-UP WAY (Song 7:10–13)

Love poetry reflecting the openness and vulnerability of real love.

- Did this poetry embarrass you? Why?
- Why do you think people get embarrassed about deep expressions of love, but feel happy with the mass of sexual images in society?

■ **A 'LIVE FOR TODAY' SHORT-TERM PERSPECTIVE ON RELATIONSHIPS (Song 3:5)**

Wisdom on dealing appropriately with feelings for another person.

– What does this verse mean for dating relationships?

– Can you think of anything Jesus said about this? (Jn. 6:63)

After five minutes, ask each group to read out their passage and feed back what their group discussed. Then allow a further five minutes for the group to get back into their pairs and fill in the second column on the handouts: 'God's Views'. Encourage them to discuss as they fill it in.

SO WHAT?

Draw it together by asking them, on their own, to fill in the third column on the handout: 'My Views'. Play some ambient tunes and when they have finished, encourage them to close their eyes. Explain that you want them to think about the 'so what' of all this with the views they've just put down on paper in mind:

What does it mean for their lives? Which of the issues raised is their weakest – difficulty committing? Unrealistic perceptions of what a relationship will be like? Or, a tendency to swing from hot to cold? What do they plan to do about it? You might want to read out some of the Bible passages above, which seem most appropriate to the group. Conclude this by inviting the group to fill in the final section: 'Your Ideal Match' and spend a few minutes thinking about what it means for them.

WRAP

Brief your older (OAP) guest beforehand that you'd like them to close the meeting by sharing with the group one piece of wisdom about this whole area that they've learnt during their life. Ask them to close by praying for the group.

MEETING GUIDE:

Sex – How Far Can I Go?

Author: Steve Adams

MEETING AIM: To consider an alternative question to 'how far can I go?' and look instead at 'how close can I stay' to God when sexually tempted?

WET PAINT

10 minutes

As the group arrive, have a piece of wood propped up somewhere visible with a notice 'Wet Paint – Do Not Touch' next to it. Prepare the wood just before the meeting so that the paint is clearly wet. Use a bright coloured paint (water-based is preferable – it will come off fingers more easily than gloss). Don't draw attention to the wood or the sign, but when most of the group have arrived, pop out the room. After a minute or two, stick your head back in and say, 'I meant to say, please don't touch that piece of wood. The paint on it is a special kind and can have a strange effect on anyone who touches it'. Then disappear again for another few minutes. (You can use sweets instead of paint, if your group have a sweet tooth!)

Officially start the meeting by asking if anyone touched the paint when you were out the room. If not, ask whether anyone was tempted to. Why?

Produce three signs, one saying: 'Don't touch what you haven't got', the second 'Always keep your feet on the floor' and the third 'Don't lie down together'. Place these on the painted board for all to see – they will stick to it as long as the paint is still wet.

Then say that we are going to think about sex, and how far you can go in a romantic relationship before you are married. These three phrases are often used as guidance to stop young people going too far. But do they really work? Or are they like wet paint signs having the reverse effect, making the thing being banned more attractive?

Allow time for any discussion this sparks.

GROUP VIEWS

Split the group into smaller clusters – about three people in each. Give them five minutes to talk about these questions:

10
minutes

- When you see a sign saying, don't walk on the grass, don't touch the wet paint, or don't talk, why do you often want to do what you're being asked not to?

- When someone gives you a task, what motivates you more – them giving you things to aim for, or them telling you what not to do as you start the task? Why?

- Do you give up sprinting more quickly when you're running away from something, or when you are running towards something? Why?

Come back together and invite each group to relate some of their discussion and conclusions.

Bring out the point that in anything we do, we'll be more motivated by 'dos' than 'don'ts'. And, over time, we'll have more energy for things we are aiming towards than things we are running from. Try to give several examples from your own life. Before the meeting, ask one or two of the group to think about examples from their own life. Give them the chance to share here.

GOD'S TEACHING METHOD

Give out Bibles and explain you are going to look at the teaching methods God employed with Adam and Eve. They must listen out for any point in the reading when there is a 'do' or 'don't' – not necessarily the actual words 'do' or 'don't', but any examples of God forbidding something or encouraging something. As soon as they think they've heard one, they must shout

8
minutes

out 'do' or 'don't'. The reader then stops while they explain what they heard. Keep a record of how many are picked out.

The readings are Genesis 1:26–31 and Deuteronomy 10:12–15. After the readings, total up the scores and read them out – the 'dos' should outweigh the 'don'ts'. Don't interpret the results – simply invite people to comment on what they think this says about God's teaching methods.

HOW CLOSE CAN I STAY?

Refer to the phrases 'Don't touch what you haven't got'; 'Don't lie down together' then ask:

■ What other phrases have you heard which relate to boy-girl relationships?

■ What do these focus your mind on – God, or the sexual temptation you're trying to resist?

■ Are these negative, or positive? Do they motivate, or hinder?

■ Have you ever found an answer to the question, 'How far can I go?'

On a large sheet of paper write out the two phrases above as well as any they have mentioned. Also, write the question, 'How far can I go?' Suggest that the thinking behind these phrases and question is wrong. It focuses the mind on the temptation that you're trying to resist, not on God, and it's designed to get you as close as possible to the (pleasurable) temptation without actually sinning.

Put a line through the question 'How far can I go?' And write next to it, 'How close can I stay to God?' Suggest that they start to focus their thoughts on this question the next time they are tempted sexually. Give out slips of card with this question on it.

YOUR CHOICE

Say that God has given us the freedom to take our eyes off him and what he wants. In Adam and Eve's case, it was when they did, that things went pear-shaped...

Get a volunteer to read Genesis 3:1–6.

Drive home the fact that God has left choice in our hands by playing a short extract from *The Matrix*. Show the clip in which Neo is taken to meet Morpheus for the first time. Morpheus offers Neo a choice, represented by two pills – a red one (using the power of his choice for good), and a blue one (using the power of his choice for bad). Play the clip, stopping at the point where he swallows the red pill. Then ask:

■ If you were in Neo's shoes which pill would you choose? Why?

■ In a situation of sexual temptation, if you take the red pill, and try to do the right thing, does it get easier, or more difficult?

■ From experience or your own hunches, what happens if, in your own life you choose the blue pill?

Conclude by explaining that God does offer us the power of choice. He wants us to choose the red pill, to choose to run towards real life, and him.

Have a bowl of blue and red jelly beans then do the following:

Hold up a blue one. Explain that when we are in a situation in which we might sin sexually and we are thinking 'how far can I go?' we are taking our eyes off God and putting them onto our own sexual desires. It's like we're eating the blue pill and using our choice for things God doesn't want for us.

Hold up a red one. Explain that when we are in a situation in which we might sin sexually and we think, 'how close can I stay to God?' we are eating the red pill and using our God-given choice to do what God wants.

Give them a red and blue jelly bean each to take away as a reminder of these choices.

MEDITATE

Get the group in a circle and play some background music. Invite them to think about how it might change things if the next time they face sexual temptation they forget the question 'How far can I go?' and ask themselves, 'How close can I stay to God?' Give out copies of the worksheet and explain that they should fill in answers to the questions posed on the worksheet.

10 minutes

Close by passing round the pot of red and blue jelly beans. Invite everyone to take the colour which they know represents where they are at. Encourage everyone to eat the sweet as an honest confession before God of where they are at, and to talk to God about this. After five minutes, pass it round again. Invite everyone to take the colour that represents where they want to be. Again, allow five minutes for them to eat the sweet and talk to God.

MEETING GUIDE:

Violence

Author: Chris Curtis

MEETING AIM: At first sight, a youth meeting on violence might seem straightforward: after all, violence isn't something that Christians generally approve of. However, the subject isn't as easy as it seems. The aim of this session is to get your group thinking about what they believe, and applying it personally. They may make discoveries about themselves that they had no idea about before.

So, by the end of the meeting, your youth group may not know or understand everything about the Christian view of violence, but if you send them away with a little more knowledge, some new questions and a desire to think it out for themselves, the meeting will have been very worthwhile.

YES, NO, MAYBE

This exercise is a chance for your group to start thinking about the subject of violence. The aim is to get their gut response to a variety of situations involving violence and decide whether they think it is justified.

10 minutes

Give each member of the group red, orange and green pieces of card or paper. Sit the group in a circle where they will be able to see each other's responses. Then read out each of the situations below and ask the group to hold up the card that best represents what they believe. If they feel that violence is acceptable in the situation, they should hold up the green card; if it is not, the red card; and if they are not sure, the orange one.

You may want to stop for discussion after each situation and allow the group to comment on their views and the views of others. Try to avoid violence breaking out over any disagreements!

- a man hits someone who insulted his family
- a heavyweight boxing championship fight
- a father and his children are attacked in the street and the father hits back to defend them
- a WWF wrestling match
- a pupil hits a teacher who is aggressive towards them for no reason
- a teacher hits a pupil who is aggressive towards them for no reason
- a US soldier kills an Arab fighter in the Middle East
- an Arab fighter kills a US solider in the Middle East
- a man hits someone who is trying to steal his mobile phone
- a man is sentenced to death for murdering his children
- a woman smacks her children when they have done something wrong
- a man threatens violence to a drug dealer who is dealing to children in his town
- an old lady hits a burglar over the head while he is trying to steal from her

WHAT ME?

This next section is designed to get your group thinking about how angry and violent they might get in certain situations. You'll need a balloon for everyone and it's probably best to start yourself, so everyone can see how it works.

15 minutes

The idea is to describe your nightmare day: a day when everything that annoys or angers you actually happens from the moment you get up to the moment you go to bed. They could be small things: like people dropping litter, or your mum or dad burning the tea; or big things, like being bullied at school. For each occasion, you blow a little bit more air into the balloon. The idea is to keep going until the balloon bursts.

You may need to give the group some thinking time to prepare for this, even writing some ideas down if it helps. Encourage them to include the silly and trivial and the important and serious.

After each person has had a go, ask them to say if they honestly believe there are occasions when they would or could be violent. Do they think they would be right to do so? Do they wish they could control themselves more?

The balloon also makes another point that maybe worth you mentioning: that sometimes our reaction to something, violent or not, is as much to do with other things that has happened in our day as it is to do with the thing itself.

IS GOD VIOLENT?

Now to the really controversial stuff: looking at what the Bible says about violence! Rather than giving your group some set answers, the idea is to get them thinking for themselves and searching out what the Bible says.

20 minutes

Divide the group into three teams and set each one the task of finding out what a part of the Bible says about violence.

Team 1: the Old Testament
What happens when people reject God? (Gen. 6:11–13)
What does God think about people being violent? (Ps. 11:5)

Team 2: Jesus
What does Jesus say about violence? (Mt. 5:38–42)
Are some kinds of violence acceptable? (Lk. 12:49–53)

Team 3: The future
Will there be more or less violence in the future? (Lk. 21:10–11)
Is God ever violent? (Rev. 19:11–15)

Have the teams report back to the group what they have found and see whether you can draw together any principles from what has been read. Again, don't be worried if all the questions are not answered. Encourage the group to talk, think and read about the subject. For example, maybe they could find some Bible study resources on the Internet that would help them.

VIOLENT NEWS

Hand out copies of the worksheet and allow them ten minutes to read and work through the sheet. After that time come back together and ask some of the group to read out their stories. Encourage discussion around some of the questions and issues raised in the stories.

PRAYER MAP

One of the clear principles coming from the Bible is God's abhorrence of violence towards innocent people. Finish the meeting in a quieter mode by thinking together about the people who suffer violence every day.

For this section you will need a selection of newspaper cuttings on the subject of violence in the UK. These will need to be collected over a period of days or weeks. You'll need enough to make a rough map of the UK on the floor using these cuttings. Ideally the map should be a couple of metres long.

Give the group some time to walk round in silence and take a look at the cuttings. Encourage them to read them. They represent the violence that occurs around our country every day. Once everyone has had a chance to take a look, ask them to select one story that has made the biggest impression and pick up that cutting. Then give a chance for group members to pray, either quietly or out loud, for the people and situations they are looking at.

Finish the prayer time by reading out loud the words of Jesus in the Beatitudes (Mt. 5:3–10).